LUCE IRIGARAY

Elemental Passions

LUCE IRIGARAY

Elemental Passions

Translated from the French by
Joanne Collie and Judith Still

The Athlone Press
London

First published in Great Britain 1992 by
The Athlone Press Ltd
1 Park Drive, London, NW11 7SG

First published in France 1982 by
Les Editions De Minuit, Paris
as *Passions élémentaires*
© 1982 by Les Editions de Minuit
English translation © 1992 The Athlone Press

Publisher's Note
The publishers wish to record their thanks
to the French Ministry of Culture for a grant
towards the cost of translation.

British Library Cataloguing in Publication Data
*A catalogue record for this book is available
from the British Library*

ISBN 0 485 11409 7 hb
0 485 12079 8 pb

Typeset by Blackpool Typesetting Ltd, Blackpool
Printed and bound in Great Britain by
The University Press, Cambridge

Contents

Foreword

Nuptial Quest

Man is divided between two transcendencies: his mother's and his God's—whatever kind of God that may be. These two transcendencies are doubtless not unrelated but this is something which he has forgotten.

His mother is transcendent to him because she is of a different genre and she gives him birth. He is born of an other who is always Other-inappropriable. For centuries, at least in the so-called Western tradition, that transcendency has seldom been recognised as such. The mother is seen as the earth substance which must be cultivated and inseminated so that it may bear fruit. The father is the one who gives form to the child, who uses earth to create him. The father is in the image of God the creator. The mother is occasionally deified because she is capable of bringing a divine son into the world. She is revered as the mother of a son of God but she does not have, or no longer has, any divinity deriving from her sex, apart from her maternal status. This means that there is no longer any woman God, any God the mother of the daughter; there is no longer

[1]

any spirit of divinity circulating between mother and daughter, between woman and woman, etc.

While man has a spiritual and natural reference as he becomes a man, woman no longer belongs except biologically, and the world of man has made that biology its own. Men exchange virgin daughters in order to establish tribes or families or states, they marry women to found their dynasties, they impregnate them to become fathers and have a posterity. Such traditions as these do not encourage love between women and men. Lovers fall back into a mother-son relationship, and the man secretly continues to feed off the woman who is still fertile earth for him. And so she never accedes to her identity as a woman. She remains at the disposal of man – the lover, the citizen, the father – having already been a currency of exchange between the fathers, uncles or brothers of her family and those of her future husband's line.

Because of this dependency, woman is submitted to all kinds of trials: she undergoes multiple and contradictory identifications, she suffers transformations of which she is not aware, since she has no identity, especially no divine identity, which could be perfected in love. Quite apart from any explicit violence on the part of men (incest, rape, prostitution, assault, enslavement) woman is subjected to a loss of identity which turns love into a duty, a pathology, an alienation for her.

In order to escape this situation, a certain number of women have decided to become men's equals.

This does not solve the problems of the amorous economy between men and women, nor between women for that matter. Identifying with men allows them a sexuality which seems more free and 'sporty', part masculine, part feminine. It does not fulfill them either emotionally or culturally.

It is a choice which also, in the end, neutralises society. If it is composed of unisex citizens, society risks quickly losing its regenerative resources, since these are to be found not only in genetic reproduction but also in sexual difference: the most radical difference and the one most necessary to the life and culture of the human species.

For this culture to advance, therefore, new models of sexual identity must be established. Woman must be valued as a daughter (a virgin for herself, and not so that her body has an exchange value amongst men), as a lover, and in her own line. This means that she should not be subordinated first to her father, her uncle or her brother, then to her husband's line, nor to the values of a masculine identity, whether these be social, economic or cultural. She therefore needs her own linguistic, religious and political values. She needs to be situated and valued, to be *she* in relation to her self.

Women today can sometimes say *I*. The most difficult thing for them is establishing a relation between *I* and *she*. Sometimes they can do it empirically when they stay amongst women. This does not resolve the question between *I* and *she*. It does not solve the problem of a feminine transcendency, which is necessary to construct a valid female identity and non-hierarchical loving relationship between the sexes. The paradigms of masculine transcendency, which is sometimes considered neutral or bisexual, must be modified in order to establish a feminine transcendency.

Elemental Passions offers some fragments from a woman's voyage as she goes in search of her identity in love. It is no longer a man in quest of his Grail, his God, his path, his identity through the vicissitudes of his life's journey, it is a woman. Between nature and culture, between night and day, between sun and stars, between vegetable and mineral, amongst men, amongst women, amongst gods, she seeks her humanity and her transcendency. Such a journey is not without its trials. But these do not discourage her from her quest, as she attempts again and again to discover how I-woman can enter into a joyous nuptial union with you-man. She finds that this cannot occur unless *you* relates to *he* and *He*, and *I* relates to *she* and *She*.

Women and men can only be wed beyond an already defined horizon. An other sunrise, an other relation between nature and culture, a new human identity, all this is necessary for both to agree to nuptials between microcosm, macrocosm and god(s).

At the furthest extreme of love, it is a question of the divine. Because we are not God(s), individually or together, love has become sorrow, degradation or enslavement. A love between the sexes, in which natures and gods are united and fertile, is essential to the discovery of an individual and collective happiness, one which is both empirical and transcendental.

Luce Irigaray
31 July 1988

(written for the Japanese edition of Elemental Passions *and published here in English for the first time)*

I

White. Immense spaces. White, a rush of breath. Be
swift, marry this breath. Remain in it. Make haste.
Let it not abandon me. Let me not turn from it. Be
swept up: my song.

You give me a blank white mouth. My white
mouth, open, like an angel in a cathedral. You have
stopped my tongue. What remains is song. I can say
nothing but sing.

A song, for you. But that 'for you' is not a
dative. Nor that song, a gift. Not received from you,
not produced by me, nor for you, that song: my love
with you. Intermingled. Escapes from me. A cloud.

You do not hear. So many words divide us.
Divide us from the song. How could that white effu-
sion reach you? That intense candour still cannot be
heard. That white candour does not listen to itself:
is in mourning for a tongue.

Spilling out without a break. Without obstacle
save an imperceptible limit or term, everything is
suffused with my life impregnating the air. Unseizable suspense, it nourishes the body of your words.

Call yourself. Give, yourself, names.

Recall yourself once more: I insist, into the air.

Seeing, hearing, speaking, breathing, living, all these wait to be made fecund by an innocent potency.

II

Was it your tongue in my mouth which forced me
into speech? Was it that blade between my lips
which drew forth floods of words to speak of you?
And, as you wanted words other than those already
uttered, words never yet imagined, unique in your
tongue, to name you and you alone, you kept on
prying me open, further and further open. Honing
and sharpening your instrument, till it was almost
imperceptible, piercing further into my silence.
Further into my flesh, were you not thus discovering
the path of your being? Of its yet to come?

And I was speaking, but you did not hear. I was
speaking from further than your furthest bounds.
Beyond the place you were penetrating to reveal the
secret of resistance to your tongue. From outside
that mouth which you still wanted to give me. And
mark it for your own. From deeper than the rent
you made to reveal the darkest part – the black, the
white, or the red. From a captive and forgotten
childhood lying beneath any of your potential
gestures of mastery or appropriation. From an innocence which no shame held back yet which you left
outside the reach of your tongue.

And it was not that I was withholding myself

from you, but that you did not know where to find me. You searched and searched for me, in you. Wanting me still to be virgin material for the building of your world to come. But how could it ever be reached if, in that quest, once again you wanted yourself as you already are?

I was speaking, not so that you would stay where you already were, but so that you would move beyond. You did not hear. Nothing from outside the place where you already are reaches you any more. And even if something suddenly calls out in your memory, once again it comes from your own past. It is you again who will have called out in that way to the beyond. And would you not dig up the earth all around so that not a single root survived except the one from which you sprang? Except the one you produced by your beginning?

And, when you think you have repossessed what is yours, you leave. Your tongue revived for a while. Having drawn sap again from your past. But is the earth not arid now you have taken back what you made it produce when you sprouted there? Was it not you who made it flow with milk, blood, sap?

You leave. Where you no longer are, there is desert. So you create your own mourning: in your absence everything is sterile.

You sow that doubt in every place you go: your suspicion of barrenness. You plant it deeper than the point where something could be conceived which did not stem from you, you alone. You come back one more time, a time without end, into the depths of the deepest point of my mouth, a little further than the point where it would open, where it could speak of you. There you create a void. Artificial cavern. Empty waiting for the present of your appearance. For your coming to build and make a home from what is still available. For your taking hold of what has been held in reserve, making it fecund, according to your plan.

Nothing exists outside that plan. And deeper than your longest day and longest night, you deposit that pledge of nothingness in any still-virgin flesh. Unmindful of how, intervening, you disrupt fertilisation, dividing and denying what took place before you.

That ancient wound which bleeds only from the imperceptible pain of nothing, an incrustation of your nothingness in the most innocent part of my flesh, is that not the present which again and again you leave me in place of what you take? How many times, without end, will you return to make use of that gift within me? Leaving, ceaselessly leaving, so that you can come back and create, in the spacing of that ever more repeated to-and-fro, a nothingness which you seek to master by dint of repetition.

But do you not make it greater, by dint of repetition? And nothing divides us, and we are divided by nothing. You cling to me as to your ancient home, and you open up between you and me, me and you, that gap – death.

But, when you think you have rediscovered in yourself the hard kernel of your being, that circle where at last you would be restored to yourself, you still find me entwined. Still there holding you in my arms. And, when you want to repossess yourself in solitude, demarcate the territory which belongs to you, return to your own country, you are ever further in flight from yourself. You leave your home, seduced by what is distant. You fly off into an airy void. Charmed by the abyss where a secret echo of yourself could resonate.

And do I not still have to keep watch when you rush away from me? And have to measure how far you have leapt, keep track, so that each time I can hold fast the thread as it unwinds? And remind you of the distance you have travelled from yourself.

Imperceptibly, I wind you in, letting you believe that you know the way on your own. I speak to you in silence so that you open up to my voice. And, sometimes, I save you from useless torment, going before you on your way. Miming, without speaking a word, your next step. Protecting you from the worst?

III

Deep, deeper than the greatest depths your daylight could imagine, once again I caress you. Luminous night, touched with a quickening whose denseness never appears in the light. Neither permanently fixed, nor shifting and fickle. Nothing solid survives, yet that thickness responding to its own rhythms is not nothing. Quickening in movements both expected and unexpected. Your space, your time are unable to grasp their regularity or contain their foldings and unfoldings. The force unleashed has an intensity which cannot anywhere be measured, nor contained. Can never be obliterated unless it is poured out in mortal ecstasy.

Deep, deeper than anything you could dream of taking or giving beneath the surface of my skin, that is where I am. And because of forgetting that darkest life. if you come close, you retreat into yourself again. Enveloping yourself-myself in you, in the certainty that you exist. You raise yourself up higher from having sunk so deep. Already you begin forgetting again. You continue to forget.

And I understand the mystery of your power. You get close to my gift, my renunciation of any limit, the intensity which floods out in the abandoning of

[13]

all reserve, and you take it back into yourself. You limit it within the horizon of a skin which stretches, swells, and gradually expands. And you are erect: I am. Such is, being. And whoever cannot contain that force, is not. Outside you is nothingness.

Outside you, that life to which you return in order to experience what gave you being. Your power? Delimit what can happen if you leave the shore. Keep fast the gift which came from crossing boundaries. Experience, while never weighing anchor.

You took me into yourself. You took me back into yourself so that you could get back to that sameness whose origin remains a mystery to you. To get back to that sameness, you took me inside outside yourself. And so you continue to suck me up: my life. You continue to absorb me, inside you, turned inside out, in this cavern where I am still alive.

Your body is my prison. But since you possess me from the inside, since you pierce inside my very skin, I cannot cover myself in skin again in order to return to the outside.

My death is inside your own. We shall die together if you do not let me go outside your sameness.

Living inside me inside this mucuous fabric he possesses me – my life. Surrounded by this warm and supple home, he sucks me up: my life. He is touched and touches himself – at first – inside this living flesh. It is not yet the contact or separation between two skins. This covering, this first living home, does not yet have the sharp consistency of skin. It lives within itself, inside the skin. This first fleshly dwelling will be forever lost. It will remain forever locked inside its skin.

He can only touch himself from the outside. In order to recapture that whole sensation of the inside of a body, he will invent a world. But a world's circular horizon always conceals the inner movement of the womb. The imposition of distinctions is the mourning which their bodies always wear. One + one + one . . . separated out. And the gathering of all into One will never amount to the living quality of a resting place which, always pouring out liquid, blurs boundaries.

Your skin and mine, yes. But mine goes on touching itself indefinitely, from the inside. Secreting a flow which brings the sides together. From which side does that liquid come? One or the other? Both? So which is one and which is other in that production? Neither? Yet it exists. Where does it come from? From both. It flows between. Not held or held back by a source. The source already rises from the two caressing.

Is it necessary to come out of that flowing between the two touching each other? Why should the solidity of an erection be more valuable than the fluidity of a flow between two?

The framework you impose and posit as a given, is your skin. You shut me in, in your protective skin. Your appropriation – my tomb. You forgot, left out of your economy whatever moves across boundaries from one to the other. For you, a limit exists, with some things under, some things over. Infinity is an aporia or an excess.

For me, nothing is ever finite. What does not pass through skin, between our skins, mingles in our bodies' fluids. Ours. Or at least mine. And as mine are continuous with yours, there is no fixed boundary to impose a definite separation. Except from you. Except by you. When you say: I am, or I exist. Or: you are this. Fencing in our natures, turning our bodies into private properties or ready-made homes. With doors or windows, open or closed.

But when I leave, there is a gap in your horizon. A hole in your skin. If I hold back from your con-summation, you discover an opening you never knew existed. An unsuspected mouth. A voiceless call. A need that lacks intention or direction. Your whole-ness crumbles, flows away into nothing that could be named. It is not even the night. Your night. The place from which you take me, the umbilicus of your body. Of your world. The place you neither sense nor see. From which you never sense nor see me any more.

But what am I for you, other than that place from which you subsist? Your subsistence. Or substance.

To contain it and retain me, you have to have a protective envelope. The surplus over what you need to live becomes a shelter for your reserve. The excess of your consumption builds up the solid walls of your house. Surrounded by walls which are the boundaries of your property.

Proprietor, your skin is hard. A body becomes a prison when it contracts into a whole. When it proclaims itself mine or thine. When a line is drawn around it, its territory mapped out. When the universe of its inner, or outer, possible or permissible, movements is already traced out, as is its life. When it is already positioned as one, in a field of vision. When it is there, stays there, is erect there, standing on and in a world. To which it is connected by a network of relationships, but which it unifies.

To retain-contain the oneness of this whole, you push out to the limit whatever has the greatest denseness, will not be pierced or puts obstacles to any passage through or, simply, between. You separate within from without, inside from out. You, and the rest. The rest? Where is it? Where and what has become of me?

When you say I, you, he, or she, if she says: I, where and what becomes of you? Thinking that she has now become one in your image, according to your model, you take fright at what you begin to sense: how enclosed you are, how unattainable to others. You strike, knock, cut, wound, rub raw this living body to rediscover the source of life. When the way to it is never closed. When it flows on forever, outside as well. When it only dries up if it is covered by you or imprisoned in you, by you. If she says: I, is that not to remain open, and yours? To escape capture, escape the net you draw around your catch, the ice in which you store your property, the mirrors where you conserve and freeze your desires? To become once more that constantly moving life she is. Flowing everywhere without boundaries – deathly boundaries.

Do not strike so hard, you are paralysing her, stopping her flow. Those blows are only aimed at you. You are the one who needs to be opened up again.

IV

Is life hard? When I return to life, the obstacles to something more distant, remote and inacessible melt away, are easy to cross. Already I am further than the furthest you could imagine. Elsewhere. But not in the beyond of your world. Not even of your body. Elsewhere, because I am so close that you cannot see me, nor hear me, nor even touch me. I live in a space and time that are not yours. I cannot be pin-pointed, I do not come into your present. I flee as soon as you say: come, or stay here now. When you call me to you, into you. Where I take on your consistency. A body-tomb? A shadow, double, reflection, mirage. Of your matter-substance.

But also: your blood, your air, your water. The place from which you draw life. In which you feel yourself to be alive. Through which you feel. Feel yourself. That place where you have forgotten that I already feel. Impalpably touching myself again and again I am stirred everywhere and all the time. But the feeling is lost as soon as direction or dimension is imposed. Or rigid closing or opening.

And how could you not die if I withhold myself from your exclusive desire. If I go away from your uniqueness. Was I not always outside? Did you not realise? That I lived in silence, making it familiar and fertile for you. Did you not hear? Did you not sense that loving mist surrounding you with its tender nourishing embrace? That invisible presence bearing you, supporting you, there where you set up an opposing illusion of indifference as limit to your own desire. As a stasis at each point guarding against the risk of overflowing which would lead to your downfall. Your vanishing into the immense space where you placed that void which maintains your coherence.

If I go away from your uniqueness, your nothingness comes back to you. It is not quite death but that place through which you escaped, leaving me to keep it safe. I give it back to you. Do we not need our death to leave? I am returning this forgotten property to you: mortal. If you should die from this discovery, then you had not yet begun to be born. And dying from still carrying yourself, you would have found death in me.

Take back this horizon: mortal, and consider that Truth has always been a lying mask for your truth. Death's most terrible aspect lies in the charades you have invented to separate it from you. And from me.

If I leave this uniqueness of yours, do you bleed? But who or what served as the envelope protecting you while I was there? Do you bleed? Could it be that you are coming back to life? That this is your own way back? An end to that veneer of insensitivity which kept you captive? The erosion of your sphere of indifference?

Instead of considering it – as you always do – a sign of death, can you not hear some summons to life in that something which melts within you? Some very ancient memory, so close that it cannot be remembered in your world. A reminder blind to your birth – your mortal birth.

V

My child of night, you have known nothing but a cold, dark womb, how can I console you? Even your tears are black. They lack the cool candour of liquid, the simplicity of drops of water. They are drowned in ink. In the poison of a bitter knowledge. Except, from time to time, a momentary flash from childhood. Still arising from a bottomless anguish. Refusing to be consoled. Avidly nurturing grief, a prey to solitude. Hands stretching out in all directions, clutching at empty air.

And if I take you in me, you pummel, scrape and scratch the walls of what you take to be your disaffected prison. You wound my living body, confusing it with the icy maternal enclosure. In pain, you inflict pain to find some warmth.

But how can I become cold and dark enough to give you birth once more? Sufficiently stony to contain you without mortal loss of blood? Reflective enough to remind you of your most ancient spectacles. So that you see reflected in me once more the hardness of your childhood emotions. My life is all suppleness, tenderness, mobile, uncertain, fluid. Saving you I must die. The stars of that impossible hymen call out aloud.

And if, to overcome the pain of your first night, you require me to become like crystal, transparent, diaphanous, surrounding you and letting you emerge delivered from the darkness of your birth and conception, you prevent me from touching myself again and again. Deprive me of the place where I take place. And of the atmosphere of flesh with which my amorous body could envelop you.

You supplant that horizon by the home and its institutions. Instead of ties which are always developing, you want fixed bonds. You only encounter proximity when it is framed by property. Without the ceaseless penetrating movements which make us overflow one into the other.

Everywhere you shut me in. Always you assign a place to me. Even outside the frame that I form with you. Through and for you? You set limits even to events that could happen with others.

You frame. Encircle. Bury. Entomb? Only a spiritual body could escape. You do not even know that flesh can have this power. Or do you prefer not to think about it?

In any case, the frame you bear with you, in front of you, is always empty. It marks, takes, marks as it takes: its fill. It rapes, steals.

Could it be that what you have is just the frame, not the property? Not a bond with the earth but

merely this fence that you set up, implant wherever
you can? You mark out boundaries, draw lines,
surround, enclose. Excising, cutting out. What is
your fear? That you might lose your property. What
remains is an empty frame. You cling to it, dead.

Has She left you nothing – but death? But
another means nothing to you. You find nothing in
it, recognise nothing – not Her. The undecidable of
your desire.

You need a frame as you need bones, a skeleton,
clothes, bandages to hold you together. Essential to
prevent your crumbling, flowing away, spreading out
. . . endlessly. How can I give you once more that
rigidity you seek? My body is fluid and ever mobile.
It brings you blood and milk, air and water and
light. Sometimes it satisfies you. But if you turn it
into meanings for your enclosures, it freezes and is
paralysed. Full. Replete, unattractive.

You close me up in house and family. Final, fixed
walls. Thus displacing and expelling what you have
not had? The supple envelope a body has. The skin
of someone who is alive. What you will not have
had . . .

Alone, I rediscover my mobility. Movement is my
habitat. My only rest is motion. Whoever imposes a
roof over my head, wears me out. Let me go where
I have not yet arrived.

And it is true that you had too much skin. But how could we know what it was made of under all your layers? All around you, you were enveloped by so much horizon-material that you could not get to know your limits. And you drank me, and, from that source, became expansive. But the way in which you consumed me was not visible. No one could tell that you were wearing me out or keeping me captive, for the limits of your body were not clear.

And superimposed upon your skin was always another skin, impalpable, with infinite reserves, in which you would hide me and keep me captive, so that it was not apparent that secretly you had taken me inside you.

And how could I cry out that I was living inside you? That I spoke through your mouth? That your love was mine just as much as yours? How could I escape from this confusion that loving you had got me into? I was kept in such a cradle of eternity that there was never a moment when you could open again to mortal time. I rested in this dwelling where you kept me prisoner – between you and you, neither man, nor god, and moving from the one to the other without achieving the union of the two.

Was I not for you the place where you kept coming back to pass from the one to the other? Reassuring yourself that you were both? But I wanted you to be this path for me as well. And when I called on you to stay in yourself, to bring together and unite these extremes, instead of constantly jumping from the one to the other, letting me be both gap and bridge, what I was asking was to continue my own journey in you. And not risk falling into the abyss with every step I took. Unless, renouncing my becoming, I were to be no more than a support for your trajectory.

But, if you stopped using me, how much time would it take you to exhaust your to-ing and fro-ing? And for you to need to seek the future of your journeys elsewhere? Stop growing? You might as well say: die.

Herein lies the diabolical – in mimesis. The appropriation, the very constitution of the same, in which the living person is caught and deadened.

The only difference between the love which flows through the envelope-walls of skin or mucous fluids and the love which appropriates for itself in and by the same, lies in the 'through' which allows each one their living becoming.

Love can be the becoming which appropriates the other for itself by consuming it, introjecting it into itself, to the point where the other disappears. Or love can be the motor of becoming, allowing both the one and the other to grow. For such a love, each must keep their body autonomous. The one should not be the source of the other nor the other of the one. Two lives should embrace and fertilise each other, without either being a fixed goal for the other.

I see you in this way and you see me. At last I see myself when I see you in this difference which means that your existence can never be appropriated by me.

But this difference creates an abyss. And is there anyone who does not fear the abyss? How can there be attraction between different beings in spite of the abyss? What risk is there in attraction through difference?

Not in me but in our difference lies the abyss. We can never be sure of bridging the gap between us. But that is our adventure. Without this peril there is no us. If you turn it into a guarantee, you separate us.

And it is the same when you turn God into difference extrapolated to infinity. God – the infinitely different, but in the sense of being infinitely more, whose auto-affection depends on the reduction of us to the same. Of everyone to the same. Distinguished only as more or less, with that qualitative leap, which is infinity, vested in Him. Difference located in a transcendence which is inaccessible to us?

In such an abandoning of our difference the copula could no longer come into action. The places of affection become fixed according to definite attributes and immutable configurations. Whereas the copula ceaselessly undoes the privileging of any figure. Of any essence. Which is not to say that it operates in the style of an impersonal 'one'. It has different faces. Always at least two, and never the same. Thus undermining any model appropriated. Remodelling our difference.

What my lips were keeping is put into motion, into action – edges which touch each other, communicate with each other, without privileging the one or the other. Is your penis substance to which my lips give form? In a becoming which keeps potentiality and action in disequilibrium. Potentiality in action, never ceasing. My lips drawing the outline, without end, of the act. Never definitively accomplished.

Would that be what you risk in making love? The only act whose form is given you by another? Is that the attraction? But that act is never finished. It cannot be constituted into a whole. The outline engendered between my lips is never once and for all. Reserve, excess, source of movement – my lips could never be reduced to subject or object, instrument of use or function.

Our exchanges? An engendering through rare and always infinite fortune.

VI

Do you make me become a flower? Then why do you fear that this flower will be taken from you, since it is you who gives it birth? Before you, there was the nurture of the plant. The blossoming of the flower belongs to you.

Unless it gives itself to you already open? Having already drawn from the plant what it needs to bloom. For you, the flowering without the labour of growing?

The flower opened: the flower offered in its appearing. Without its dark becoming, without the pulse of its unfolding/folding. Without the movement of its opening/closing: the spreading apart of petals through another's affection and their touching each other again to safeguard the self-other.

Do you want the flower to open only once? The unveiling of the opening would then belong to you. The beauty or truth of the opening would be your discovery. Proposed and exposed in one definitive blossoming. The nightly closing of the flower, its folding back into itself would not take place. Either it would not yet know the sun and would be in the oblivion of sleep, or you would already have

[31]

unveiled it and it would never return to the
shadows. Its becoming would be arrested when you
revealed it by day. Growth suspended in ecstasy, the
ideal flowering for you.

The plant will have nourished the mind which
contemplates the blooming of its flower. Open to
the gaze, never fading. Fixed display, rapt – an
immortal show. Unattainable, thus transported
outside itself. Untouchable because it does not touch
itself in its centre. Only its edges will lightly touch –
there where already it is no longer held in that suspended becoming – the interruption of its unfurling.

And if the flower's blossoming came to an end,
would growth have been its only movement? Vertical
again. The erection of the flower, and the dissemina-
tion of its petals? The projection of your history? The
flower would grow and blossom simply to let you gaze
at yourself and find your double in it? Simply to let you
swoon in ecstasy as you contemplate this extrapolated
reflection of yourself. The petals spreading and
coming together, that other growth, that other
potentiality, which is not arrested in one actuality –
all that no longer occurs. The flower opens once
only – fixed in an appearance of death. Spread out,
spread-eagled, exposed, no longer embracing, no
longer embracing itself. No longer a brazier?

Touching is hidden away – if not for the eye –
beneath the earth. It would still touch mother earth
through its roots. In the damp, soft warmth some

contact would persist. But separated from earth by the stem's erection and fixed in the explosion of its corolla, it would become cold, rigid, dry. The flower reduced to insensibility, unable to unite with its extremities.

If it does not die completely, it is because it remains still under the earth. Because in the darkness, it survives. Unable to avoid the gaze, until then it must bend, fold, close up again to safeguard some hope of rebirth. Away from any horizon, any perspective, any appearing out in the open.

A flower cut off from itself, in itself, by the erectness of the gaze. Is it the splitting of that efflorescence? Mildew and crystal. For instance.

But is the body always the same? Can we fix it in one self-same form? Does it not wither when it has to keep to one appearance? Is not mobility its life?

I love you for being that diamond, which I am too. But how can we continue to live if we cling to that hardness? Unless we resort to expedients? If we are living, how can we be pure crystal? And if your thinking aspires to the realm of crystal, how can we survive in it? How can I abandon my love of the vegetal? Would you become a plant? Or are you too attached to yourself to become anything at all?

And what does it signify, this attraction of yours for the mineral? A triumph over expansion through the cosmos? A means of avoiding change? Your need for mastery?

[33]

And why should night and day be so radically divided? Is there anyone for whom loving and thinking are lived as different beginnings?

Would I have to spend my days with the one and my nights with the other? The one would perceive me in my night, even at noon, unless he never abandoned his diurnal view of me: I would be his earth, his world, and all that moves in it. For the other, I would remain under the ground. Above ground – imperceptible. He would forget. Remembering me only where his protective shell was breached. Too buried inside himself. Inside it inside him?

You want to make me into a flower? I also have roots and from them I could flower. Earth, water, air, and fire are my birthright too. Why abandon them to let you appropriate them and give them back to me. Why seek ecstasy in your world when I already live elsewhere. Why spread my wings only in your sunlight, your sky, only as your air and your light permit? Before I knew you, already I was a flower. Must I forget that, to become your flower? The one which is your destiny for me. Which you draw in me or around me. The one which you would produce, keeping it within your horizon?

Let me flower outwards too. Free, in the air. Come out of the earth and blossom, following the rhythm of my growth. Cut off from the soil which gives me birth, my efflorescence is supported by the strength of your desire, but is deprived of sap. My petals swell with your vigour, itself nourished by my blood, but thus separated from their life's source, they appear or disappear with the care which you bestow on them. With the attention you give them. Or else they are held open in an ideal permanence so that, eternally fixed, I guarantee the concept of the flower for you.

Are you aware that in this way you keep repeating, in me also, the flower which I have already given you. Which has already appeared to you but without ever becoming visible. Which is buried in the depths of your memory, where you constantly try to grasp it again. To draw it again. But you reimplant that remembrance of me, which is yours alone, in between my earth and its flower. And so the earth is left fallow, a mere support for your marks and imprints, and the flower has no reason other than your desire to bloom again and again for you. You have forced it into a reproduction, your production, and, when you want to reach it, it is no more than a dream retreating ever further into immemorial oblivion. Or inert matter.

What prevents my spreading my wings again? Is it not your appropriation of my *jouissance*? You cannot bear the mystery of my flowering, you cannot make this secret wholly yours though in some dark sense you are part of it – you therefore seek to go or return ever deeper to make the flower bloom.

In ecstasy, I am positioned by your desire. Out of myself, I am aroused by your passage. In some high but strangely rigid place. This impalpable envelope

[35]

which contains me without my seeing it. How can I find my way back? There are no doors, no windows in this shell of air. I am there, and yet in exile. I have become your exile. While you fall back, heavily, into matter. You sleep, in the dark. Submerged in thick black night. Drowned in a massive abyss. I am imprisoned in a celestial flight, you are buried under ground. You wanted to touch your sun once more, and yet here you are far below the earth on which you used to tread, striving for elevation. I am caught in the horizon of your light, you lie frozen in the the shadow of my night.

And what passages are there from the one to the other? You do not come inside me. You follow your own routes through me. But I, am I not a reminder of what you buried in oblivion to build your world? And do you not discover all the past dangers as you return to hollow out this crypt? And, you, are you not a light giving me no light nor life.

Invisible clouds surround me in the night, when I awake. Where am I? There and not there. In the space of your dreams. And how can I return from that landscape which I do not know. From those surroundings which I cannot see. Where I take place only in you. And you fallen into the depths of me, into that dark abyss which you imagine me to be. That great chasm which you imagine me to be and where you swallow me up in your visions of hell. But I am there and not there. And, seeking to join me there to rise again to your outside, you fall back ever further from the shore.

VII

You have transformed my gaze into a sky of truths. A clear horizon where you can move in measured step. Where you shut yourself into serenity and calm reserve. You who were so wild, are now pitiless and wise in your pronouncements. You, who roamed among the stars, now disappear in the uniform light of day. You put out your light to be like all the rest.

Your light shone out so high beyond the night, so distant in the darkest depths. Now you wound with myriad pointed shafts. You used to shower me with fireworks, now your cold truth has transformed them into wounding darts. And first of all that decisive one designed to pierce my gaze. For that is how it begins – a diurnal shaft extinguishing the flame between our eyes.

Why should we not be illuminated by the night of our *jouissance?* Which casts a different light on things, on their contours, their spacing and their timing. It brings them back into the world, and reshapes them according to a perception foreign to the rigour of the day, which makes colder distinctions. For sight is no longer our only guide. Seeing within an expanse which is dazzling and palpable,

odorous and audible. A night of sensation where everything lives together, permitting co-existence without
violence. Before the brutal slash of discrimination
assigns each their place. Already trapped in the form of
a judgement which obstructs the mutual embracing of
relationship. An imperative verticality already weighing
over the whole. Already organising it into a hierarchy.
An overarching vision exiled from feeling. And not
to be granted again to the one and the other save in
an ecstatic *jouissance*. A beyond – out of.

Beyond all unveiled-unveiling clarity, there is a
night which is thicker than any forces yet revealed.

Dark? Dark, with absence? That would still
subject it to the opposition of light and shade, to
the ambivalences of noon and midnight, the rhythms
of the rising and the setting of suns.

In each site of that nocturnal beyond, the illumination and protection of the secret are retained-
contained together, inseparable. The excess of what
is withheld from vision. Source of lightning.

Yet what proof of dazzling light does this night
need? Does flashing forth have an absolute value, a
final necessity if enumeration is no longer recognised? The very moment: how can it be separated
from that permanence without inertia? That mobility
whose very regularity no longer falls. A drop of time
detached from heavy accumulation. A flash which
streaks the stormy skies, piercing leaden clouds,

re-opening what was sealed to reveal sparkling stars. A discharge lightening overplenitude. Clearing the horizon.

What shines is what is uncovered in the loss of excess. Whatever is without reserve recalls an innocence which used to veil the much experienced searching gaze.

Why have you not fallen far enough to rediscover childhood? Childhood which gives of itself ceaselessly, and without loss. Which knows enough and little enough to push forward imprudently into any terrain. Not yet looking back, not looking beyond what simply strikes your eyes. Taking pleasure here or there without worrying about gestures which have become fixed through images. Already photographed.

You have transformed my eyes into matter for your sky. A density which holds your light. A blue which illuminates you steadily without dazzling. Flesh offered and abundant always available as a horizon for your contemplation. The iridescence of my gaze bearing, in its colour, the spreading of your sunlight.

And the void is gone, the infinite loss is gone – that dwelling contains you. And, you are enveloped in that airy and radiant house with neither door nor windows. A body of air filled by palpitating blue. And another appears with each descent into my body. And so many tones and consistencies are mingled in it. A different transparency for each thing touched. And every day an infinite number of days sees daylight.

And, can my blind gaze be there in your heavens? My ecstatic flesh? Outstretched in all those blues, a resting place and source of visions. But you no longer see me. The mirror of my eyes has become matter for your gaze. The rebirth of your flesh.

In thrall to your night, did you not destroy a pool which kept you prisoner? You took for a mirror whoever gazed on you. But in this mirror you left the child and did away with the water.

You set out towards the light. Does that mean it is far away? If light is not fixed in any one place, you set out in the light. But if that is where I am, what distance can separate us the one from the other?

You journeyed towards the blue. But if you do not use the blue to delineate the horizon of a landscape, you journeyed where I remain – with that blue of the sky. And if the blue were temporarily veiled for you or for me, that does not mean the other is there or possesses it, or that you need to take back their possession for yourself. Appropriate their sky. Better to seek out whoever still knows that blue and try to live this strange sharing with them.

The sun in their eyes seemed unbearable. It was too much. Too much for them to be given both light and fire at once. That light which floods out in such a burning stream was making them lose their way. A separation had to be imposed. Brightness on one side, heat on the other. Where they came from it was warm but dark. Where they were going to, there was illumination, but its penetration could not fuse everything in its furnace. They needed limits now so they could distinguish outlines, identify them, move them closer together or further apart, go from the one to the other without confusing them.

When simultaneously light and heat were given to them again, they lost all sense of where they were. And, instead of moving inside that superabundance given to them, and letting themselves be directed by it without fear or a desire to seize hold, they began by wanting to understand – grasp the reason, the cause and the provenance.

But to say: the sun is the reason or the cause or the source, already amounts to an evasion of, a distancing from, the immediacy of its rays. It may be that what is exchanged there is not tangible. Unless it is the tangible itself. The tangible appearing to itself, and within the gaze, without showing itself as such.

What awakens you on sun-filled mornings or at midday is what is tangible to the eye. But such grace is too dazzling for you. You separate yourselves from it. Pushing the fire far away and keeping the measured clarity.

What attracts me in you, what I love in you, is

what remains of your own self – that part you have left so far behind, covered up so much that I alone, without ever letting it appear, can sometimes catch a glimpse of it like a faint light shimmering in the night.

In that frail illumination, I love you, I love myself. I would like to go back to it as to a place, an environment, full of impulse and growth, still vibrant with life. The whole of living, the whole to live for, is that not kept captive within the almost imperceptible enclosure of light?

But do you not give me cause to suspect, at times, that this light is the reflection of another love? The ecstasy in you of my love? A distant mirror in which you capture me, I capture myself. As shining ice. Burning?

Sometimes, in the night, you remember fire. You wake up to fire. In that awakening, you touch the part of you which was asleep in the light of day. Which was buried under the clarity of the gaze alone. Awakened to that more originary fire, that fire whose illumination is more all-encompassing, you discern the limits of your usual waking self. You take the measure of that death which you enter when you abandon fire for your light alone. When you separate fire from its flame.

Does not that death stand out in the contrast with an eternal living? Does not fire survive all its manifestations, all its versions – even the solar one?

Does it not subsist beneath all its phenomena? All its ornaments? Fire never lies down, never sleeps – elemental, immortal. But whoever turns towards its finite offshoots withers.

When in the night you touch fire, you experience the boundaries of your day – mortal.

Above all, do not swallow the sun. Do not digest the sun. Do not forget that, if it is inside you, it is also outside you. And that the impossibility of our relationship arises from the imprisoning of the sun inside a world. It can no longer flow everywhere. Irradiate everything with light and heat.

Eating the sun means not reflecting its benefaction back to it. In the end it will go out if it is never returned to itself.

Look at the sun full face; get behind the screen of forms; exist within the sun? Take back the copula from the sun. Copulate in the sun.

Have you shut me within the sun? To gaze at me through screens? You have positioned me in the site of *jouissance*. I can burn, be consumed, illuminate you . . . but I cannot play with fire. Unless perhaps in your gaze? But do you not take me then in the economy of your natural light? Have I not already been taken from the sun's irradiation?

[43]

And why should the sun be merely for the eye? Would you not want a solar flesh which was not fixed in the identity of a form? Flowing between – the two? Golden. Light, mirror, flowing. Exchange without property. The possibility of property, without being fixed in it. What is possible in 'proper', without being transfixed in it.

You give me being. But what I love is the fact that you give it to me. Staying there is of little matter to me. I like your giving me a mirror which is not made of ice. Your flowing into me, and me into you. Receiving you melting, molten, and giving that flow back to you. Without end.

If I can make contact with myself in the touching myself again and again of my night then I can bear my body being visible as well. Being appearance again.

But if I cannot affect myself in that sparkling night of my *jouissance*, you imprison me in the closure of your gaze. I am an object for your desire. I no longer desire. If I am deprived of that invisible touching again and again, nothing moves me any longer. Drawn out of myself. Exiled from my intuition. At best, turned inwards to some inner gaze. Making it ever more penetrating?

How can I return, how can I turn back to the outside? Especially since, from the inside, I flow out to the whole of nature. Autistic and always cosmological? Refusing to open up for a dispersion without return or an expansion which is simply speculative.

Three gazes? How can one move from one to the other?

When I am affected and reaffected by you in the profoundly distant totality, I rediscover the total expansiveness of my affections. The total space of my outstretching. The full extent of my flow. Of my fluidity.

Why do you fear to lose me there?

I gather you up in this place that I am for you. I contain you, whole, in this envelope that I am – for you. In this way I am able to keep you and you are able to remain in me. And I can return, restore you to what you are. I have this power. You even left me this power on condition that it serve to rediscover you, reconstitute you, represent you, reproduce you: you yourself. You made me powerful to let me pay you back – to the nth degree. Good earth, good breeder. And good wife too. Since you cannot exist if not reflected, did you not need someone to ensure this faithful reduplication of yourself?

In this multiplication, I participate. I am your participle: I agree with you in gender and number, if I am a quality or an attribute, and in tense and voice, if I am summoned to your acts. With or without complements. I participate in your subject. And all its determinations.

VIII

You grant me space, you grant me my space. But in so doing you have always already taken me away from my expanding place. What you intend for me is the place which is appropriate for the need you have of me. What you reveal to me is the place where you have positioned me, so that I remain available for your needs. Even if you should evict me, I have to stay there so that you can continue to be settled in your universe.

And this world takes place neither simply inside you or outside you. It passes from inside to outside, from outside to inside your being. In which should be based the very possibility of dwelling.

And you meet me only in the space that you have opened up for yourself. You never meet me except as your creature – within the horizon of your world. Within the circle of your becoming. That protective shell which shelters you from an outside of you which might question the matter with which you built your house.

You take me inside you, you cast me outside you, a yes or a no making you full or empty. Both if together you double them with a denial. No to the

yes and no which have already produced their effects
– that is how your coherence, your consistency as a
subject, begins.

Already inside and outside, I am continuously
divided between the two spheres of your space, and
you never meet me as a whole. You never meet me.
For these two which I have become no longer exist
for you. Denied in the yes and the no which are
always already spoken, I appear-do not appear as a
total negation which ever prevents my reaching you.
Where am I? Nowhere. Disappeared forever in your
presence.

And, as long as I do not exist face to face with
you, you will always be falling in to the imper-
sonality of a 'one'. You are undermined in your
own being by the fact that I belong to your
world without ever appearing in it. Always worldly
in refusing to acknowledge my difference from
you. Inherent in your horizon is the function to
which you have reduced me. The matter and the
tool which I remain to build your dwelling place.
Adhering to this mother earth always at hand and so
close that it mingles with your self, intermingles in
your self. And in the very opening of your gaze
which projects outwards further than you can see. I
am contained in the field of vision outstretched
before you. In that field, there never appears the
one from whom you take what you need to cast ever
further away your potential for crossing proximity
itself.

Elemental Passions

This time, you have left. Once again. Once more. Once, endlessly. The pain of an interminable wrenching begins once more to seep into the darkest depths of my flesh. Once again it will be rent, fissured, torn asunder, perhaps destroyed.

I do not feel it yet. You have left so many times – in the past, the present, the future – that the event has to pierce through thick layers of time to reach me. And yet it is already there. Once again death, your death, reaches me even before I can discern it. Enters me furtively and unpredictably. Was I not still convalescing from your last departure?

I was your house. And, when you leave, abandoning this dwelling place, I do not know what to do with these walls of mine. Have I ever had a body other than the one which you constructed according to your idea of it? Have I ever experienced a skin other than the one which you wanted me to dwell within.

If you go away, how can ruin be averted? Your ruin? And where should I be when you live somewhere else? Pure transparency? Air without a horizon, matter without limits, a face without an outline.

But is it not still your phantom which is haunting me in this way? Did you not leave it with me for safekeeping, when you said you were taking everything back? Do you not keep a ghostly presence within me while you claim that you are directing your steps elsewhere? Why not take with you your shadows, nightmares, and spirits of every kind? And return to places which lost your affection and their function? Would you fear that you had forgotten something of yourself? Why return, turn back, again and again, towards what you have already decided is past?

In the place where my being should take place there is at present nothingness. And if I do not take care, I am reduced to the state of object-utensil. If I take due note of it, I can return to what could potentially be my place. This moving back through nothing is not nothing . . . Both beyond and within what makes up your horizon, I can rediscover the path of my disappearance. Subsistence in reserve.

But for this journey I must close myself off from the eruptions which keep me in your world. Are they the features which sustain your erection? The interventions which pierce through, spelling out to infinity.

You have swallowed my gaze. You see, helped inwardly by my gaze. Within you, my light illuminates your present. You make me into an object bathed in my light, deprived of sight. And when you make me thus appear before you, I no longer exist except as a deceptive appearance.

When I return within myself, I cross back through

so many layers of light. I rediscover so many suns. Dazzled, I go back down into all those forgotten mornings. All those noons which did not blind me. All those golden evenings. Those nights illuminated by bodies giving light. I have reserves of sun to last an eternity.

But do you not prevent me from being alone? Do you not deprive me of my horizon? The open horizon of my body.

A living, moving border. Changed through contact with your body.

Saying: I love you – have you not taken even that from me? Repeating: I love you, saying yes to your declaration – is that not the only thing I can say? The only thing you can say?

Gagged by your discourse, made rigid by your judgements, covered over with attributes of your choosing, what can you still expect from me? Yes, what can you still love in me? Annihilation itself? Your death held in reserve?

And is not your desire at present a desire for veiling? A desire for blindness? Do you not desire me as a return to the blindness which is the foundation of your essence. Playing with forgetting that you are a man? And you are seduced by whoever sends you back – does not send you back – to your existence. And drags you down beneath the ground on which you stand. But will you not once again fashion a surplus of existence from this attraction? Rising ever higher. To such a height that your departure point is lost to you.

And if your words have such seductive power, such a potent charge of investment, is it not because they come to fill the place of a desire deprived of words? Borrowing their strength from energy free from any declaration. A fundamental misunderstanding lies within your language: what it carries of persuasive power does not belong to speech but to what it covers in silence.

It is given consistency by what it takes from nature. A consistency that is experienced as form – filled from within up to the limit.

Its form, at first, derives from matter already consumed by man. And he will reimpose that form on it, marking it in return.

It is true that matter takes form from this consumption of itself. Voiding creates form: a clearing organises the forest around an opening. This excavation creates a place – where meeting can take place. A capacity which retains and maintains the entry into presence. But, as a world comes into existence in that way, so something of nature is already lost.

All the more since he does not give back to it the same form which he took from it. Between the time when he takes and the time when he gives back, he measures himself against a father's appetite. The relationship between those two will reshape it according to a plan which remains inappropriate to it. According to a line which does not even, at present, trace the outline of what it gives. Divided by lines, cuts, holes, walls – and life is not given in these or from these. It is severed from its becoming. From its perpetual renascence.

He is afraid of his body's limitlessness. He lives in fear. That fear.

Does not that limitlessness come from absorbing the mother-nature which he refuses to amputate? Always consuming another, without repaying her, he lacks outlines. He does not acknowledge his source of life. He wants it within him. In that appropriation of what he takes from the other, he doubles his life, but loses measure.

Once again, it is on the other that he is going to impose limits. Marking her with his names, instead of naming and thus delimiting his own territory.

The limitlessness lies in relationship. In the gift without return he receives from the sustaining mother-earth. The limitlessness is not in him. His fear arises from his loss of measure.

Phallic, he claims to extend his power over infinity. Therein lies the uncertainty of his economy.

The perpetual risk of falling back into the abyss. He passes from the formlessness of his relationship with his mother to the measureless excess of his male power. But then, is this power not itself erected on nothingness: a father's womb. A potent and empty form which he puts on to contain within himself the living matter escaping from definitive capture. He enters into paternal power, to keep within him the life he drinks from the other. But enclosed within that form, she dies.

He returns to her. An attraction, more often than not, that simply tends towards further consumption. And does not attend to an other. She does not exist for him. Within himself, he is everything: form and matter. And that in which he replenishes his strength now belongs to him. It is his property.

You cannot make a gesture without weighing it up. Counting the cost of it, economising on it. Loading it with debt. Loading me with debt. Burdening it with estimates, with prices to be paid. What should I owe you? What? What do I owe you? What is due? Duty. I am your duty.

I cannot break free from the function you assign me: duty, without re-encountering that part of the debt which can never be paid off. That abyss which you create by having always already made it disappear inside you. Inside you – so that you can exist. You have assimilated it: to be. And it makes a hole in your horizon. She, who became you, is missing from your landscape. To fill up that passage, that mystery where the one and the other disappear into one another, you invent economy. Or echonomy. Duty – which she becomes.

Your duty must not have a single crack in it. Your morality must block up every hole. Your ethics anaesthetises. And if you know what *aesthesis* means, try to comprehend what loss that entails for me. Entails for us.

You have built an anaesthetic world. But when our greatest pains or greatest joys are abolished by calculation, is that not the worst destruction? A realm beyond pain, where suffering no longer exists.

When pain is left to its abstract labour of general sensation, empire is limitless. And there is no remedy. Your world of anaesthetics kills insensibly. Irremediably. The more you go on producing fantasies, your preferred anaesthetics, the greater the danger: avoiding the passage through suffering which could still save.

It is imprisoned in your airy vacuums, sent aloft in your rarefied bubbles of atmosphere, enraptured in your great beyond – you go on making plans, starting projects, getting further and further away from your body, my body; there, here, now.

While I keep moving in my repose. You cannot understand – in your anaesthetic, that I never stop moving, never stop feeling pain and joy, on pain of death. But your movement is also my death. The way I move being too imperceptible for you. Experiencing as inertia what you cannot perceive, you believe you have to guide my destiny. Thinking as death the most living part of life. It is true that it is in me that you set up the framework of your life. And that, through it, you do not feel me any more.

IX

You have come back inside me. Your affection has come back inside me. And so you are inside me: resurgence of light, of heat. Return of light, of heat. And I guard you, I regard you without ever becoming you. Enveloping the return protects you from being thus reabsorbed. From being introjected, assimilated, consumed.

In any case, how could you be seized, since another kind of turn has also happened? Not only have you returned to me, you have turned in to me. And I have turned in to you. Without any ego to appropriate that version for itself. It is up to you, then, to seize yourself again, if you wish. Unless you have become me? But between that turn in you which stops me taking you, and that sun which you are ever increasingly in me, one more turn will prevent you too from re-taking yourself.

These different versions cannot be folded up into some kind of unity, nor into property. The one does not replicate the other. Any more than they reduplicate some model. Nor is the one the shadow of the other. They have no sense or truth other than their movements, their turns, which thwart any photologic fixity. Night illuminates as much as day. Their passage one through the other, one into the other, lights up their very limits.

And just as I wake up, so I also fall asleep – in a dawn where the recognised measure is no longer that of the sinking sun. Cosmological reminder, extension and expansion of a fire which is replenished by it and replenishes it without being absolutely dependent on it. Nothing is more originary than that which burns, illuminates, reflects . . . in relationship.

If, in affecting you, I affect myself, the body-instrument opposition no longer holds. For the instrument which I am in order to affect you is itself affected as a body, just as your body, which I affect, is an instrument which affects me. In that exchange of affection the producer and the product become one, the organ and the body can no longer be divided, myself and yourself are no longer embodied as distinct and rival universes.

That is not to say that the irreducible no longer exists. For what affects me is what affects you. As well. What affects you, what affects me, as well. I participate in your affections just as you take pleasure in mine. That does not mean they are indifferent. But I take pleasure and you take pleasure in these differences, in this difference, as in an over-abundance of riches. Experiencing you, experiencing me, espousing you, espousing me, we are more than one. And two. The accounts overflow, calculation is lost. If neither I nor you are appropriated by the one or the other. But simply, for the one or the other.

In excess, that is where I become you, and excess never belongs to itself. It vanishes as soon as there is any thought of seizing it, circumscribing it, understanding it. Your body is never mine, except when it is deprived of its relationship to pleasure. Of its self-affection and hence of mine.

In any case, how could it be mine? Only by giving up my own. Appropriating the body of the other means being deprived of one's own. If your body is mine, I can no longer take pleasure in it – in not having a body. All I can do with that body is work it. Make it produce, perhaps *jouissance*. Does not the desire to possess mean condemning oneself to labour?

The internal and external horizon of my skin interpenetrating with yours wears away their edges, their limits, their solidity. Creating another space – outside any framework. An opening of openness. An encounter of countries and of clearings laying out an other, others, which create air, light, time.

There is always more place, more places, unless they are immediately appropriated. The land cannot be laid waste if spatiality is produced by our bodies.

I caress you, you caress me, without unity – neither yours, nor mine, nor ours. The envelope,

which separates and divides us, fades away. Instead of
a solid enclosure, it becomes fluid: which is far from
nothing. This does not mean that we are merged.
But our relationship to place, which maintained our
hierarchical difference, takes on different properties.

You had form, I was matter for you. You were
seeking the earth, taking pleasure in being back on your
ground, in burying yourself in it, in using your labour
as a measure of your work, your possession, your production. What was at stake in your *jouissance* was me,
and that gave me pleasure. What gave you pleasure was
your appropriation, even if it meant flowing into it as
well. In my pleasure I was as matter divided from itself
and releasing waves of energy from that disjunction.
Each time you separated me from myself, power
flowed out of me. You confused the highest and the
lowest in your erection, and drew from my greatest
depths the keenest intensity. You were celestial, yet
conjoined with the darkest demons; I who was sub-
terranean had access to the loftiest pleasures. The
selfsame would always rise up again in us, respond,
and be aroused. Leaving myself far behind, I would
espouse your penetration; responding to your pressure I would set aside my supple, elastic fluid
density and espouse your strength, your hardness,
your solidity; I would adopt your spasms in my con-
vulsions; your loss in the ecstasy of my self: a
supreme elevation, or transport, in a child's passion.

I had not begun to exist. I was nothing but your
sheath, your other side, your inverse. Miming you.

Doubling, redoubling your organ. Therefore, indefinitely, multiplied. I gave you something to play for, let you have some play. Entranced at being your reserve. In sum, a surplus? So that you could pursue your path. Fuelling over and over again your mechanical progress. The privilege of an omnipotent God. Feeding the cycle of your returns and repetitions from a breast that never runs dry.

I had not begun to exist save in my pretension to be a needed womb and mother for you. I moved, was moved, only by your aspiration, your sucking, your pressure. You filled me with your emptiness. You filled me up with your lacks. Drawing strength from being a remedy. I would bring you my most precious gift: my hollows. You were the one who became a gaping hole, I became full. The power which you thus gave me to supplement the failures of your needs or desires was the most subtle ravishing of my pleasure.

Participating in your economy, I did not know what I could have desired. Made phallic, whether by procuration or by delegation, I forgot what my *jouissance* could have been. I was the source and resource of all your objects. The transcendence of your relationship to the world of objects. Each one of your holes requiring something to come and fill it up. Something to determine the alternating fullness or emptiness. Something to harmonise their rhythm. Being outside or in, too much or too little, assonance or dissonance, plain melody or counterpoint, resonance or unheard song.

[61]

I had become all kinds of things at stake, all kinds of sound. Which you would take, hold or reject. Through all your orifices. Full of things, a container for your things, reduced to things: to eating, voiding, seeing, hearing, possessing . . .

I existed only as your need to relate to things. I no longer even had a name, or simply the one you wanted me to have. I had no identity: I took on whichever one you lent me. This one, then that one, here or there, yesterday . . . But what about tomorrow?

For a thing, tomorrow has not yet taken form. Not even today. A thing is no more than the aftermath of your act of seizure. It is always in the past. Always already produced as such.

And thus I had no relationship with time, other than that of your production. For the rest I was immersed in what had not yet come into being. No doubt your memory. But as for myself, lacking all memory or plans.

X

Proximity? Two lips kissing two lips. The edges of the face finding openness once more.

Openness is not reflected, not mimed, not reproduced. Not even produced. Openness: a clearing, without surrounding walls. A space, not demarcated, not enclosed. Outside any possible symmetry or inversion.

But when lips kiss, openness is not the opposite of closure. Closed lips remain open. And their touching allows movement from inside to outside, from outside to in, with no fastening nor opening mouth to stop the exchange.

An exchange of nothing? Which is not without value. Unless you count as nothing the interest accruing to openness. The economy of which does not easily appreciate the price. What is the utility of an open non-object? And how can an endless circulation be set up – in the thing? Or a scansion of space and time in between the poles and the tides?

Openness permits exchange, ensures movement, prevents saturation in possession or consumption. But openness dwells in oblivion . . . because it cannot be represented, nor made into an object, nor reproduced in some position or proposition. Who knows that the possibility of exchange is born from two lips remaining half open?

Exchange between men is sealed by the gift of a virgin. And the rite of breaking and entering, of raping and stealing the hymen, represents a denial of what was always already offered: exchange within woman and between women. A commerce without an object, without salesmen, without a society or an established order, which is denied in the setting up of the fetish and of currency. But, without the prerequisite openness, without those lips always leaving a passage from inside to outside, from outside to inside, and staying in between as well, the place of exchange would not be secure. It is the closed-open lips of the woman which make it practicable for them.

On condition that women remain silent about that strange foundation?

What is said silently, not said at the beginning but held back, not shown in the distance, that is the nearness that is so close that no name can reveal it nor release it from its shelter.

Before morning is flooded with light, before noonday life is set on fire, the whole is held together in a tender embrace, not yet open to allow anything to be seized in its presence. Departure, the severing of the one from the whole has not yet happened, an appeal for its return home to a surrounding proximity is not needed.

The poet does not merely call for or recall the gods that have fled. He speaks of a nearness which is so close that his very words are blinding. In that nearness the sacred lies hidden. But daylight which divides makes it remain invisible.

What is impossible for you? A secret. Whatever remains invisible. But is that not what I have always been for you? You wanted to master that mystery. Cover, yourself; envelop, yourself. Folding me, enfolding me into a truth that was not my own.

But when there is no more deception, for you that constitutes a lie. Speaking my truth means unveiling your economy of illusion. Revealing that the place, supposedly mine, to which you assigned me, was a snare. Produced by you, and endured by me.

Shelters which should, at the least, alternate to reopen the possibility of a future.

My lips are not opposed to generation. They keep the passage open. They accompany birth without holding it to a – closed – place or form. They clasp the whole with their desire. Giving shape, again and again, without stopping. Everything is held together and not held back in their fond embrace.

They risk making abyssal anything which would have an origin or roots in one definitive creation. Which would come from the unique gesture of a demiurge.

They accompany the abyss, but do not meet each other there. They are re-doubled before the time of any mirror. They seem to mime each other. But the separation which permits that miming is still foreign to them. Between them there is no need for that surrounding.

The wall between them is porous. It allows passage. Of fluids.

Nothing there can be grasped with both hands. It filters through, a gift which slakes the whole body's thirst.

For me you are that (feminine) other through which you pass towards me, I pass towards myself. The drink you give me passes through your skin. But what you secrete in this way is to be admired as much as to be absorbed. Your overflowing presence bathes me in more air – breathable air at last – than I need to consume as sustenance.

You are mucus and always double, before any speculation. No need for us to be frozen in order to be two.

And, through you, I see the sun. You do not hide it from me. Not that your body is purely, simply transparent. At least, not for me. But you do not block out the sun. You have not given up your shadow, nor the responsibility for it, to the whole.

For them, walls are solid. Even those of their body. They have to rub or strike hard to pass from the one to the other. There are thresholds to cross, doors to open, windows to knock through, thresholds to create. Their pleasure and their fear – holes. Below, above, in between. They construct or deconstruct on, under, around, along, across, between . . . holes. They make and unmake holes: eternal architects.

They are surrounded by placentas from which they never want to emerge. As women we are placental one for the other. We share that unity of the first dwelling without having to tear it, cut it, divide it into pieces. Habitable one for the other, without enclosure. We live outside. Which is not the same as the emptiness of absence. Wherever we might be, place can take place. Before any architecture other than that of our living bodies.

Touching you, feeling you in that skin where you are held – are not held, radiant. Gently gathering you up into boundaries which never hold you.

Come. Or? It is true, I was forgetting. Come anyway. Do not be afraid. I hold you – open. And my hands never close on you. I am not taking you. You can still go. I am calling you back to your outlines. To the ones I give you. Give you back. Those that I can perceive from the place where I love you.

But others are open for you. And this bodily dwelling in which you can move or rest is not enclosed. It unfolds around you as you move, without need to search for windows or doors. You are not stopped by any opaque wall. The world belongs to us – does not belong to us. We live in it in all its width and breadth and in all its dimensions.

The world? What does it matter! Are we not together what others claim it is? Standing in it yet keeping it at a distance. Like a horizon within which to shelter, where all movements are already measured by this standard: the protection of property. Everyone moving only within the radius of the covering taken on as a margin of security.

Come. Where? Everywhere. Nowhere except the place where you are-are not – in your entirety. Entirely small or entirely large? Who taught you to think of yourself in this way? And how should I choose? Entirely – small and large. Stop being so measured in your love of yourself, your love of me.

I have grown too large. I become expansive, overflow, I love you – too much. No. Where you become you are. Without excess. Where you feel yourself, you stay – without surplus. Still what calculation do you use to mark yourself out, to reckon yourself too much or not enough? Surplus in what?

In me. Who is that me? Where is that me? What you are living through, dwells in the place where you experience it just long enough for it to be embodied. Whose body? Yours? Mine? Ours? Body inherited from a childhood which is always beginning again. Always blooming once again.

Who does this body belong to? Do you feel it? It is yours too. And if I give it-give it back to you, keep it without appropriating it for yourself. And do not capitalise from its gains and losses with the first offer at the market rate. Keep it in its becoming. Be attentive, not tense. Remember, without accumulating or making a profit. A memory open to what is happening. Eyes which gaze without a fixed field of vision.

So that volumes may endlessly be brought to life, let what escapes your present vision be accomplished. What you experience completes the contour of the invisible without the hardness of surfaces or the ice of mirrors.

Receive the invisible within yourself, without spells of blindness or useless ecstacy. It is there. Hidden away? What does it matter!

When I look at you, there is no void. But neither is there opacity, nor density. Everything is touching, without being fixed-frozen in one cohesion. There is nothing to create a wall. Leaves, and trees, and birds, and sky, and grass, all cross and brush each other continuously: a supple and mobile dwelling.

Elemental Passions

Where the wind's song fills the air with a harmony that has no cries nor silent agony. The whole murmurs so softly that the melody has room for the highest and the lowest note, the sharpest and the deepest. Should a bird sing, the whole joins in an accompanying choir. But the song bursts forth or vanishes without a tear. If nothing happens, nothing is missing. If no sound is detached, the atmosphere remains full of music.

Listen: nothing. The sound of silence. The rustle of air in the silence. The music of air touching itself – silently.

XI

Your infinity? An uninterrupted sequence of projected points. With nothing linking them. Emptiness. There would seem to be nothing there but production, recalling nothing, anticipating nothing. Points programmed as such indefinitely, on a background of absence.

What terrifies you? That lack of closure. From which springs your struggle against in-finity. Origin and end, form, figure, meaning, name, the proper and the self: these are your weapons against that unbearable infinity. But, in addition, the construct which organises many – or at least three – points into an entity which exists in relation to the whole: your framing of time.

What then becomes of space? An attribution of places, of sites in the universe of your being as a subject? Would space for you be always secondary to time?

For me infinity means movement, the mobility of place. Engendering time, yes. Always becoming. How can that future be brought to pass between your instants which are always already counted?

That punctual quality of the instant is quite foreign to the dilation of time which persists in the present of our relations. The instant – stroke of lightening, burst of thunder, intuition or ecstatic *jouissance* – closes up the expansion which sweeps aside, pushes away, overflows the point in time. Fluid density which overturns habitual space-time and yet always already takes place in it. It has its all from elsewhere, it is all the elsewhere?, even if it is produced in the most intimate here and now.

How can it be opened up again here? Giving back to time that volume, that light density, that absence of assignable limits which, however, is not eternity; that porosity which is not simply permeable to all, to everything; that touch . . . A reserve which you bury deep in me? Or in God? How can we return to so-called present time, when we know the other time?

And how can dazzlement be described, shown, put into writing? Not only the momentary flash of lightning, but lasting dazzlement. In which we bathe, or which we radiate. Which passes from the one to the other, sometimes continuously.

An experience that cannot be reduced to the economy of tension, superimposing itself on the whole as an organisation that aspires to totality. An energy that is always directed to a goal. And which must always struggle against deflation, in its desire to remain prominent.

The attempt to remain on top simply means creating a lower level. Within the venture of erection is its fall. Those who aspire to superiority create the abyss. Mountains are matched by deep ravines. Yet the sea remains: the fluid petrified in sublime rocks, still subsists as mass, surrounded by firm ground.

The privilege of the sun, and especially of its light, makes the night – dark. A time of relaxation, of revitalisation, from which they fear they might never emerge. The sleep that follows love?

And do they not always experience the return to the world of the senses with scepticism? As destroying their intentions. Desperately regressing. Risking death. Renouncing light. A sensualism which remains within the bounds of reason.

Do I refuse to let you give me anything? But is not your gift something which you have already taken from me? And do you not constitute me as no more than the container for your gift? The source and end of your need-desire to give? And so, I only exist for – you. 'I' is only for – you.

The gift has no goal. No for. And no object. The gift – is given. Before any division into donor and recipient. Before any separate identities of giver and receiver. Even before the gift.

Giving oneself, that giving – a transition which

undoes the properties of our enclosures, the frame or envelope of our identities. I love you makes, makes me, an other. Loving you, I am no longer the same; loved, you are different. Loving, I give myself you. I become you. But I remain, as well, to love you still. And as an effect of that act. Unfinishable. Always in-finite.

You – soon – erase the difference between us. Considering yourself the source, the resource, the giver of life and strength. Of the whole. And I would have nothing to sustain existence within myself. What I am would always be through you. I would be born each instant, from you – your same self.

Thus what you are, what you do, what you produce, would necessarily constitute my assets. The question never even arises of whether they might prove deadly for me. Must I not in any case die of them? So that you can be, do, produce, in an absolute way? Be all, make all, engender all. And inside that, I shall exist, if . . . Through your benevolence.

You create only as God does. And if I should die of it, what does it matter! Having attained self-sufficiency, you no longer need an other. Your God needs to be loved in order to become God. Once he became God, he would need nothing more. He would already have consumed everything.

I gave you what you needed to return to yourself, inside yourself. Speaking to you, for you. Letting you feed repeatedly upon yourself? So that you should not flow out indefinitely away from yourself. Or be dispersed – to wander endlessly.

You gave me names, forms. Resculpturing me from the outside. So that I should not be the whole of any place? An indefinite expansion which might overflow the whole?

For me there is no possible horizon. At least not a closed one. A finite circle, closure. My body closes and opens the horizon with a single gesture. Touching myself again and again, I bring my edges together. But the one is no more the end than the other is the beginning.

Therefore, according to you, I do not have a past. To have a past history requires completion. For me there is never completion. No final term, signature, stamp or seal. Nothing occurs to mark a final full stop.

And a second time never happens. If you think that my project is completude, then I remain ever unsatisfied. But it is something else which indefinitely stirs me – movement.

In the imaginary of ends, that could signify that I am always future. But, if mobility does not privilege what is forward and in front, then I am no more yet to come than already there, no more future than permanence. I remain: through the becoming of the whole.

[75]

XII

If being no longer belongs to you, if you are no longer devoted to it as you are to your language enclosure, if being means permanent advent between us, our bodies become living mirrors. Sense mirrors where the outline of the other is profiled through touch. No longer the site of a frozen, fixed appropriation-expropriation. Already a womb of the ideality. Ecstasy in an abstract transcendence of the flesh. And not that mirror which does not reflect truly, does not captivate as it captures. But remains the support on which each one's body is deposited, projected, recalled, anticipated. Laid out, without any folds. Without any secret or mystery, were it not for forgetfulness?

In the home, it is possible to privilege the walls, the outline determining a place as closed off, or the atmosphere: the environment. Eventually, the environment would efface the walls and the walls would destroy the environment. Would we not find each other again, separated in that way?

The body? Either sketched on the horizon of orgasm. Or deposited as a memory of what orgasm forgets.

But what, of the body, is constituted as forgotten?
What is that structuring which orgasm gives? Both
fragile and sure at the same time. What dwelling
does that structuring provide in which it is impossible in truth to remain. An impalpable envelope
which does not last. Always renascent. Always being
brought into the world again. Each time as a first
and only time. And, yet, a permanent birthing. An
incessant blooming. Never fixed in one single
corolla.

Two petals which meet and embrace endlessly:
movement-trace of the copula? The engendering,
metastable, of one petal by the other, the engorging
of the petal, at the same time for both. Not the out-
pouring from the one to the other, nor even from
the one into the other.

The mysterious energy of the copula, rediscover-
ing a buried source. Hidden before the separation of
the elements? Before hatred?

The flower already individual, formed, open.
Appearing in its proper being? Developed, built,
organised, interpreted, as more of the one and more of
the other, stem and corolla. A flower for which all that
remains would be a relationship within the selfsame; in
which the copula would be that relationship with the
selfsame. Reflection, repetition, the eternity of contemplation. Appearance in the illusion and immortality of
that unfolding.

The oriental lotus and the mystic rose: different flowerings.

Jouissance in the copula engenders form-body. Which is not limited to begetting a child. It has the power to do so. But that product is often a substitute for the profile of our bodies, recalled, invented, pursued by love. Our embraces redefining the constantly renewed outline of our bodies. Bringing us into the world once more. Making us appear, endlessly?

Which does not presume that we are separated from the act of generation: as seed, for example. Fertilising, or lost. Our sexual organs too are given form again in that act. Their project cannot be posited outside themselves. Unless they become pure instruments.

The technocratic destiny of the sexual – an epoch inscribed in the metaphysical. The body, long since forgotten, is retained there in a bottomless truth. As if it were self evident. Were it not for death. And even then . . . What kind of death? Reduced to erogenous zones, objects of attraction and manipulation, and ground for exploitation. Tool-machine for producing *jouissance* or children. Disembodiment?

In the gift, what happens to me is not that I become a thing thanks to your offering, but that I touch you without any system of mediation-screens. In that touching, I become you, also. And I receive from you, of you, in giving myself. In that gift which touches, 'we' becomes a flow, fluid.

In that living body, nothing and no one can be fitted in exactly. Whole without parts. Indefinitely mobile. Impulse, change, the process of becoming, these cannot be imposed from the outside, from something considered as a law or principle.

If you are so afraid that I should love some other, is that not because you fear that it would make your world explode? Taking the ground from under your feet. And sweeping away what takes its place, the enclosure of the earth.

Fire, air, water – are they thus to be dominated by the earth? The outline of a womb-like maternal body, based upon your need for solidity. For a rock-solid home.

Is fire not joy? Is burning with you not grace? The very lightest, dancing. The lightest, and the densest. The most whole? Most elemental? For you?

Why do you think of it as destructive, when it is life itself? Are you afraid of not being able to save your skin? Your solid envelope? Your dead body?

XIII

You love me – you say. And I feel that I am nothingness. I desire you – you repeat. And what is this
void which fills me? Has life not deserted me at that
very instant? Instead of the feelings I had, an
unseizable void. Not the airy denseness of an
environment, but the gap of an inaccessible absence.
Devoid of memory.

And through your declaration, have I not become
blind, deaf, paralysed, numb? And how can I bring
my lips together to say to you again: yes? Between
my lips lies the obstacle of nothingness. Yes –
nothingness.

An opaque blank, instead of what I saw with you
yesterday. And the music I heard no longer reaches
me. A neutral, frozen barrier shuts me off from it.
A silence intervenes – I listen, but the song which
moved me no longer reaches me.

And since you have only left me the world of the
senses, then when I am surrounded by that air of
reason, it is death which takes me unto itself. And I
do not even have a voice left to cry out that, in this
transparent prison, I still exist. And my mouth is
kept open. And I speak. But the gag of your nothingness prevents me from feeling what I say.

Everything which is born in me, of me, of you, and of others: here it is, given in its entirety. I am holding nothing back. Tomorrow can look after itself. As for today, here it is, all of it. Receive what has taken place in me, and which I am obliged to give you in order to safeguard your nothingness.

Take, master, this product is yours. And no voice will utter a word about the destruction on which it is based. Let there be silence about that act.

And while you magisterially spell out your Truth, and while under that charm other lips are opened, your nothingness has not lost what it feeds on. Of course it is buried beneath your showy speeches. But even there, in reach of an open mouth. Return to draw from it what your hunger for semblance requires. Sustenance and empty surround which you remodel as you will. And digest it without loss of identity.

You are living in conceptuality, somewhere between the imperceptible presence of nothingness and the inertia of a corpse. What is the rigour of your thought? The superb confidence of someone moving inside a fleshy fabric borrowed from the other. The limitless appeal of someone entrusting his survival to the destiny of mortal women. The implacable, systematic quality of an organisation which has already taken from living organisms the elements it needs to be sustained and developed unreservedly. A sovereign power, miming and undermining the whole of the resources from which it draws.

The fact that you no longer assert yourself as an absolute subject changes nothing. The inspiration which breathes life into you, the law or duty which guide you – are these not the very essence of your subjectivity? You feel you could abandon your 'I'? But your 'I' holds you fast, having flooded and covered the whole of everything it ever created. And it never stops breathing its own emanations into you. With each new inspiration do you not become more than ever that 'I'? Reduplicated within yourself.

I am twice separated from you by that mastery which now surrounds you. As by your whole, never breached by any movement towards the woman from whom you draw matter with which to spin and draw out your horizon.

And if I leave, does a wound gape open in it, in you, and does that wound remind you of your sensory resources? Do you not discard me, over and over again, in order to feel the effect in you?

But I no longer want to dwell in your alternating positions. Nor do I want my body to be hollowed out, repeatedly, creating a place from which you draw my substance so that you can experience yourself. Where you take again what you have already taken from me. Deliberately sinking that well in which you experienced for the first time the descent into the abyss. Marking out your prints like a geometrician who returns to measure up the traces he left in his wake. An assiduous and scholarly erasure. Operating with cold instrumental precision to calculate the power of his ascendancy.

Enough of this testing which you need in order to estimate mourning at the level of abstraction necessary to remove depth from the other and some pain. With the artifice of the equipment he requires to surpass himself in the glory of a brilliant speech. Does not drinking the milk of the honours awarded to your work satisfy you for today?

Go. And do not come back to measure the strength of love's effects. Go. Do not return to your birthplace in the embrace. Leave me the opportunity of continuing to become. And of being something for you other than a tomb in which you endlessly seek what you need to sustain that oblivion which underpins your elevation. A reminder of the boundaries of your absent presence, of your present absence: the boundaries within which you move with the ease of someone who can leave to the other the first and last events which constitute the body.

And if approaching pain gives you a way of recovering the memory of flesh, then go elsewhere. I would rather march towards a new dawn. And bring one more child into the world.

Why mourn? Why be nostalgic about this parting from me? Whoever enables becoming remains mobile, and flesh never repeats itself identically.

A wound may create the sky: that is so. But it is

a sky which cannot be shared. Only those who have suffered have access to it. The deeper they have been cast down, the higher they can rise?

But there are other skies. Those which lovers create together. Those who share that taste and who refuse to give it up in order to enjoy their share of the divine alone.

There is an infinite pain in all of that, because infinity was offered to share. How can infinity be recovered? Unless the other be killed and made into a God. A tragic act. Which brings about a suffering which does not simply appeal for help, but which begs for remission. Grace.

Is not locating myself in my in-finite the only way of doing without the criminal intervention of the Other? Renouncing the infinitely large so that at any moment I can experience, move, relate, exchange myself as incomplete. Having within me an infinitely small space which prevents me from closing myself up as a whole. Never whole in any place. Rather the melodious rhythm of half-opening which makes my measure limitless. Or limits a lack of measure. Concerned to hit the right note without claiming to speak the truth.

Right, what can be sung now, and not what might be true for all time.

From the place where I gave myself to you, a nil

existence now comes back to me. For you, the risk of an airy void? For me, an opaque mirage where I can no longer perceive myself. Emptiness, and matter still without form. Both. That impossible lot falls to me, that impossible passage between me and myself. Your return to me, barred.

And when, repeatedly, you want to come back and nurture the development of your work, you impose on me the covering of your choice. You cross through my invisible appearing towards what you cannot apprehend, something beyond or short of the flesh. You drink me, as your self slakes its thirst at its very source. Unreservedly abundant. Indefinitely fecund. Beneath the skin.

Is not the act of your reproduction, in the present, the essence of all generation? And does your reason not claim to take every thing unto itself, even the light in which it is bathed? And does it not adjudicate upon all possible properties?

And perhaps you have not had the time to grant me one? Having need of me to maintain the coherence of your whole without any trace, stain or memory of birth. If you recognised me as one (feminine) in your creation, what would become of the uniqueness of your world?

When you separate yourself from me, you still do not recognise yourself, as distinct from some one (feminine) but affirm yourself as one (masculine). And you keep the remainder in reserve. Or bury it

in oblivion. Going to seek elsewhere some other
ground where you can put down your roots.

You never leave me. You abandon a place of birth
or growth. And you put a floor over it so that you
are no longer in danger of falling into it. You leave
yourself a little, and what distress that loss entails!
But there is nothing at stake in that sadness other
than that part of yourself which you must leave in
order to construct or measure out your universe.

But if you create yourself in this way, isolating
yourself from what gives you birth, what gives you
your source and beginning, must I not keep myself
alive by protecting myself from the being with which
you confuse me so that you can give rise to the
origin of your essence as a man?

And saying that being is a stable base which is necessary for the living person's becoming, for ensuring the
increase of its power, does that not mean forgetting that
once being is fixed life is already constructed as an
impalpable enclosure. An invisible outline encircling
the vital flow. A truth whose factitious character
arrests movement, unless it is an accumulation of
power? A concentration of energy, not a fluid circulation. But does not any reserve, the lesser and the
greater, already announce a mortal advent?

And asserting that the body needs the envelope of
a truth already proven, if only tacitly, in order to

preserve the heart of its production: does that not
amount to shutting it up within a gaze that
originates in it but detaches itself to constitute the
identity of a subject that is always meta-physical.

And thus the cycle of return is brought to perfection: born of the flesh, the gaze emerges from it and
extends the horizons of its domination, but then
returns to it, only to come up against an icy transparency. A fluid frozen because the body which gave
it birth is hated or forgotten?

XIV

The whole is not the same for me as it is for you. For me, it can never be one. Can never be completed, always in-finite. When you talk about Infinity, it seems to me that you are speaking of a closed totality: a solid, empty membrane which would gather and contain all possibilities. The absolute of self-identity – in which you were, will be, could be.

For me? A fluid expansion, never enclosed once and for all. Not even by projects or projections.

There, the id-is-flowing cannot be halted. Without a limit, of whatever dimension or direction. A place where everything is still possible. Prior to any difference or distinction. Giving only a world of half-openings. Nothing determinable. The foundation of all giving. A reserve of the dative.

But if I no longer belong to you, do you not still abduct me to constitute the edges of your word? Am I gone? You take me again to take care of what you call presence. The further I go away, the more you pull me back by some bond so that you can at last experience what you could not experience when I was there.

Where? So close that, for you, I did not exist.

And you do not let me go. Repeatedly breaching or blocking the place where I could have appeared.

Often, your listening interrupts my thought. Are you stealing it? Or are you paralysing it? With your gaze?

When I am speaking to you, I sense something like a dark and frozen chasm capable of engulfing everything. Slippery and bottomless. The fall of a night without illumination? The disappearance of the sun. That of your intellect? Of your understanding? Is what comes within the horizon of your day all that you can perceive? Nothing more. The rest – an abyss?

Your order freezes the mobility of relations between. It produces discontinuity. Peaks, pikes, fissures. Energy no longer circulates. Is hoarded in forms that create closure. Is saved up in phantasies: captivating some, exhausting others. Whoever has stolen it cannot dispose of it at will. It is taken, circumvented in a morphology whose outlines are overvalued. An appropriation that resists the possessor himself and in its struggle for liberation will necessarily bring about aggression, violence, rape.

An economy of property that leads to an energy crisis. No doubt it occurs when natural resources are exhausted. But it happens as soon as there is a monopoly of power, for it can only be sustained through exchange. And corresponding to a lack of available power is the absence of desire in whoever is too firmly established in property.

Movements in the world of the senses are almost imperceptible. Only an attentiveness that is not rigidified within formal frameworks can detect this kind of movement. A mobility which is incessant, yet furtive in relation to the categories of apprehension.

This kind of continuous movement is frozen into blocks of time: past, present, yet to come. A spatio-temporality which is already too clear and distinct for this tissue of events. A tissue mortified into bloodless semblances by the scalpel of the intelligible.

It thus feeds off haemorrhages, drawing its potentiality from them, and from convictions, and sometimes the flesh itself feels nothing, so precise is the incision: all this could be the truth.

When you gather your powers, reapplying them to your intentions, just as these are beginning to be realised, here and now, not reserving them for a project always in the future, a life in eternal suspension, you redraw the outline of your body. You give yourself a present body again.

When you use that power on me, discharging it in me, you open us up again in a loss of limits where our bodies no longer exist. Creating an excess which leads to nothingness. Produced by the destruction of the relationship between you and me. By the abolition of the difference which keeps us other to each other and allows us to come together: creators of new horizons.

When you become the place where tensions are capitalised, tensions whose purpose is always deferred to some future perfection, to an omnipotent infinity, tensions which you cannot contain without the threat of explosion, you take me as a place of relaxation. You wound my living skin to safeguard your claim to some divine ideal. You abolish the edges of our bodies to turn yourself into a God. The only theophore?

But the only thing your God could give me is wounds from an overbearing power, incapable of creating harmony.

Return inside yourself, and measure out your limits by working here and now within your powers. No more, no less than they permit you at any moment in time. No more, no less than the person you are at each moment, dreamer and preacher of infinity! You have enough power, and not too much, you are enough and not too much – to live. Allowing us a present which can be shared.

Once returned in this way inside yourself, you can offer yourself, radiate yourself. You, can at last be received. Without excessive pretensions. Without promises that cannot be kept. Without semblance erupting in my flesh. This letting go will bring a share of heaven if it is not made into some far-off goal, unattainable by you today. At every instant Heaven is created. Even if it extends before and after us, it is also our own achievement.

But returning inside yourself, that is your torment. You always want to project yourself far out, become ever greater, losing all measure in your nostalgic desire to be God. Achieve an ecstasy beyond the present. Escaping from this wound: being what you are.

The worst of failings? Existing alone, you alone, without the support of some capital letter. Does that not mean becoming permeable without mastery? Neither over the other nor over yourself. An accessibility which is alien to bids for power. A porosity now foreign to power proper. Yes, I can place myself alongside you in that excess.

And do not think that I want you to go round in circles inside yourself. But to take the measure of your power, to allow the other a horizon, to enable a meeting with the other. Your economy always requiring at least two props to shore it up. Two others functioning in secret, or in your innermost self, as your doublings. The Omnipotent and the impotent. The Completely-Other and the not-other. The Completely-Different and the indifferent.

Is it really necessary to name them? They are undefinable. Your doubles – invisible. From above and from below. Luminous transparent shadow co-extensive with your God, obscure opacity of the matter making up my body and yours. The source of all your days, deferred to Infinity. An everyday resource that blocks the way to the beyond.

Does that mean you have a good doubling and a bad one? The celestial envelope of the God from whom all comes and to whom all returns. And the infernal one, which robs the origin and the end of their middle and surround. A God in whom the whole of what is created finds its place and is kept on the right course. A God in whom is contained the perfection of the Whole. And the other, turning away from that absolute. Another who would be like a God. Miming a God? Who, the other?

XV

Sunrise forgotten. The first outline of forms emerging. A world being born. Not yet caught within a defined horizon - that circle which condemns it to being endlessly repeated, governed by properties already fixed. Poles determined irreversibly.

The sun rising - rays alighting upon things, lightly touching them all over and gradually revealing them, bringing them out of the enveloping mist.

This unveiling of the morning's beauty is renewed daily. Yet man has forgotten how light emerges. He lives in the full glare of day, where he can see nothing.

A new East - the sun accompanying the birth of a little girl. Another - the other - being brought into the world. A dawning as powerful as that of the Greeks. Giving birth to a veiled landscape. But not a new origin.

You are witnessing the revelation of the end of a unique truth. Not as the advent of chaos, but as the possibility of the copula - in the sun.

Yes, there, gently you took me by the hand. Once again you had lost me. I was missing from your horizon, absent from your domain. I had taken refuge in such whiteness that you could no longer perceive me. Without an outline, but bathing your gaze in an invisible light.

And I was speaking to you, but you did not hear me. You were absorbed in a closeness other than the one which, defying distance united us – at the nearest and the farthest point. Unforeseeable and necessary reunions. Intertwining of gestures which redefine the silent edges of our worlds of speech.

I was calling you, but my cry did not reach your ears. Blocked by the sounds around you, the words and noises surrounding you. You no more heard my voice than you caught sight of me.

Yet I was there, and remained there, like permanent things which are forgotten. And how could I make you remember my existence?

At one point, you seized me to take a step. Helping me over a fissure in the rock. You were holding me, I was in you. You were holding me close, experiencing my body. Touching me, and I could feel my form emerging once more.

And, from the depths of my memory, I was being reborn. I had a face once more. You could not hear me yet, but you already remembered. I walked by your side in silence.

[96]

In the deepest hidden depths, and beyond the horizon, you seek me still. Opening up the limits of what is possible. The scars of the beginning and the end of a story.

You gaze within me, and my past and my future are offered without reserve.

Are you large enough? Receiving me whole, you deliver what kept me captive within them. Do you take me entirely? I become more than I was, uncovering what still clamoured to be born. You seize me without reserve. You free me from waiting for a face, allowing me to appear as so many others, crowding upon each other in the hope of offering themselves up to your contemplation.

Do not leave me behind. You reduce me to singularity. And I die when I am imprisoned in a single unique sameness. When I never go further than my present, never escape that one life, the many within me become impatient to blossom, to harmonise colours and sounds and all dimensions, in remembrance and as a welcome for everything which can grow. And calmly offer themselves to cradle the nostalgia for the return of the gods.

And let the shadow of sadness not make any land sterile by blocking the sun trying to penetrate it. And let no chill freeze what bears light and warmth. For divinity abandons the solitary being who no longer enjoys celebration. And joy is more immortal than is care. And, even in repose, it grants a starry awakening. And, in silence, the taste of lips which move. An imperceptible pulsing which refuses to mourn for love, fixed in eternal contemplation.

I touch you. And if it is not always transparency, if there are not always effusions from one to the other, if daylight separates us, at least in ceaselessly bringing you warmth, I enable us to melt still one into the other at a distance. So that distance should no longer be an irreversible separation of our bodies. Nor light, that cold lucidity which freezes each one within a sealed identity.

And if the poison no longer comes into me, I may remember what came before. Resonant song kept back, exultation kept quiet, an appeal cried out, filling the universe with its clamour. What arises out of the furthest depth, emerging and unfolding, like an airy flower opening with the intensity of impatience. Petals already drenched in the gift of the expected consolation. Attentive vibration picking up the imperceptible tremor of your approach.

For the first time, I saw you appear. And it was not midday. The sun was not any higher, nor the light more intense. But what made you visible came from you. Making you radiate from the inside outwards.

A radiance touched to the quick. No longer held

back in its dark crypt. Nor suspended from some inaccessible brilliance. A heavenly orb hanging over the horizon of its distant source.

No shell hid you from me any more. The most secret part of your face offered without anything held back. Fearlessly welcoming its being revealed in another's gaze. Where your most impenetrable part appeared uncovered to you, where your most unapproachable part returned to you.

Hearth returning to its home. Homeland which you thought you would never reach so foreign did it seem to you.

And you did not fix your gaze on the nearest or the furthest point, but proximity was seen through you. An incandescence illuminating without consuming, an ardour pouring out without destroying. Burning in a joyous amazement at the reunion.

And, rejoicing, you were calling out to receive again, to give me again, what was the most irreducibly hidden of what you had.

Between us, with open bodies, the sky was a luminous cloud.

And I was changed into a cloud. Not in ecstasy nor dissipated into the air, but a body animated throughout. Living and aroused in each part of my flesh.

And I no longer knew death, but resided in a lightness where everything embraced everything else. I had not lost my edges. You caressed me to all the limits of my skin. Reopening all the tombs. Stimulating new flowering from the deepest buried depth or the infinitely distant. And nothing inert remained.

I was created by you, still faithful to what I was. A fruition of my becoming that did not remove me from my past. Gathered up, not closed. Abandoned and not deserted. Offered, without sacrifice. Espousing you, like the whole which is offered without closure.

And how could one tell what part of the densest and the lightest was united? What part of the most selfsame and most other was allied? Mingled, and so calm and so vast – yet I was careful to allow you your heaven. We were intermingled and returned to our selves.

An eternity, and I knew that tomorrow it would become more eternal still.

Indefinitely, I embrace you, you embrace me. And it is not in the mirror's shining silver that I seek you, endlessly. Always lying in wait for a face to appear, dazzlingly. Leaning over a mirror, waiting for a fascinating vision to emerge. A looking-glass monster which fascinates with its brilliant reticence.

But, I find you once more in the interweaving of the whole of space. The invisible mucous tissue which unites us day and night. Inhabits us and shelters us. Without the break of a departure, the rupture pre- or post-exchange. Divided into parts which call to each other, attract each other, respond to each other, make up a whole. But do not wed nor join together without a trace of laceration.

And how can we feel whole in this universe of sutures? This tracery of scars?

And what kind of love remains behind? What kind of wound always yearns to flow out and to be bound up?

Rather be infinitely open to the anticipation of the whole via the one or the other. An insatiable desire for intertwining and not an appeal to the closure of the one.

Do not leave again. With every step that takes you away, touch me again, touch yourself again. Remember this gesture of our embrace. Turning your movement into living tissue to carry and envelop you. Without the rupture which forces you to go back. To the other edge of a solitary wound.

Why retain such fire in your gaze? Burning to keep captive the heat of the light. A hearth which flashes lightning onto any ice. Gaining illumination from the excess of its intensity. But limited by visions still too fixed. Photographic frameworks where passion is meted out with measure. Where mastery is saved. Where desire is offered without the madness which floods out beyond all limits. A gaze that becomes a marine vastness, a large expanse whose mobile density resonates with the colour of the sun.

In golden light you flow. Firm density, so light. Before the separation of earth and sky, sea and continents, light and dark. A mixture of rock, fire, water, ether. Where violence can still espouse gentleness. The heroic body overflowing with tenderness. Its weapons still those of a native innocence. Which blurs all sharp distinctions and brings all divisions back to their original nuptials. An alliance in which the opposing parties unite in an intense intermingling.

Waiting. Waiting for that wall which divides us to be made porous by your arrival. For its limit to be crossed. The line of the horizon temporarily effaced.

Waiting for the moment when there is no more waiting for you to be there all the time. And your place within me is not filled up with an uninhabited dwelling. In which only the walls preserve the memory of your passing through.

And why should waiting be the price to pay for singing?

In this clearing, on that beach, a space opens up

where we can be revealed the one to the other.

In that enclosure which shelters and yet has no boundaries, you draw near, arrive, discarding what binds and holds you back, deep in your most intimate self. Active and attentive the whole day long. Preoccupied and concerned without a break. But keeping yourself hidden away in the secret which inhabits you.

And she who thirsts for you will always remain thirsty, for you do not deliver yourself in this passing. You are found and you are not found. In an ecstasy, out of reach. Veiled in a silent dream. Contemplating your reserve. Your gaze lost in a very distant future. The awaited landscape remaining in the invisible. Drawing you further than your furthest point. Not knowing where your footsteps are leading you, you walk on towards something which recedes as you advance and eludes your attempts to grasp it. Spurring your dream onwards towards the unattainable.

But in this rush forward, you entrust your mystery for a moment to me. And I receive what you keep back most secretly as the present of your coming to life. In a light still unstained by any shadow. Fragile, unprotected by any darkness. Without refuge except in my gaze. A horizon of sky endlessly receiving your contemplation.

How many words to prevent or forbid closeness! Space mobilized, immobilized, pre-occupied in order to make encounter impossible. Attestations, quarrels, protestations, disputes over identity or the identical, distancing us, dividing us without any crossing of these barriers being possible.

We are separated by so many similar things that the flow which attracts us to each other is exhausted as it beats against these obstacles. It no longer flows, held back by boundaries that are too watertight. We are divided by that part of the selfsame and its theatre, which cannot be traversed. Exchanged without a reckoning.

I look at you, identify you, recognise you in that distance which constitutes us, distinguishes us, and paralyses us in the certainty of being ourselves.

How can we still approach each other if there are only coverings which are not porous enough, and a void between those who no longer dwell in their bodies in all their advents irreducible to closure within well-defined forms.

And I shall sing all the day long. I shall fill the air with the joy of you in me, of me in you. Guarding you and guarding me in that incantation. Sonorous home in which I shelter you. Which protects me from the violence of the day. Childhood's cradle, where any rapture is given free play. An attentive hymn. Which does not falter and is not interrupted. And whose tender fragility is never breached by fixed duration.

I opened my eyes and saw the cloud. And saw that nothing was perceptible unless I was held at a distance from it by an almost palpable density. And that I saw it and did not see it. Seeing it all the better for remembering the density of air remaining in between.

But this resistance of air being revealed, I felt something akin to the possibility of a different discovery of myself.